Abracadabra Flute

Piano Accompaniments

Compiled by Malcolm Pollock
Arranged by Jane Sebba

A & C Black · London

Contents

Titles in brackets are unaccompanied and are not included in this volume.

1 Suo-gân	30 God save the Queen
2 Au clair de la lune	31 Ye banks and braes
3 The old shepherd	32 Thank U very much
4 Spring time	(33 Morningtown ride)
5 Clown dance	34 Scarborough Fair
6 Andrew mine, Jasper mine	35 Shepherds' hey
7 Rigadoon	36 Old MacDonald
8 Fais do-do	37 Waiting
9 Folk song	38 Fishermen's song
10 Apples and pears	39 Chimes at night
11 The nightingale	40 Kookaburra
12 Little John	41 Quem pastores
13 When the saints go marching in	(42 Love song)
14 Merrily	43 Come and sing together
15 Hot cross buns	44 Dublin bay
16 Pease pudding	45 The bear went over the mountain
17 Fais do-do	(46 Barcarolle)
18 Roses from the South	47 Summer is icumen in
19 Twinkle, twinkle little star	48 Morning has broken
20 A tisket, a tasket	49 Over the hills and far away
21 Southwell	50 Rakes of Mallow
22 Hatikvah	51 Theme from the 'Surprise' Symphony
23 The mocking bird song	52 O mio babbino caro
24 Turn the glasses over	53 Plaisir d'amour
25 Annie's song	54 Listen to the mocking bird
26 The holly and the ivy	55 Deck the hall
27 Mr Frog's wedding	56 O little one sweet
28 Away in a manger	57 Greensleeves
29 Johnny Todd	58 Where is love?

First Published 1994 by A & C Black (Publishers) Ltd.
37 Soho Square, London W1D 3QZ
©1994 A & C Black (Publishers) Ltd.
Reprinted 2003
ISBN 0 7136 6624 2

Music setting by Andrew Jones
Illustrations by Bernard Cheese
cover by Dee Schulman

Photocopying prohibited. All rights reserved.
No part of this publication may be reproduced,
stored in a retrieval system or transmitted
in any form or by any means, nor may it be
photocopied or otherwise reproduced
within the terms of any blanket licence scheme.

A & C Black uses paper produced with elemental
chlorine-free pulp, harvested from managed
sustainable forests.

Printed in Great Britain by Edmundsbury Press

This book of piano accompaniments
supports all editions, first and subsequent,
of **Abracadabra Flute Pupil's Book.**

59	The moon over the ruined castle	87	Last of the summer wine
60	Minka	88	March of the kings
61	Brother James' air	89	Londonderry air
62	Little brown jug	90	Tambourin
63	Portsmouth	91	Theme from the 'New World' Symphony
64	Huron Indian carol		
65	Hey, little bull	92	Mango walk
66	Oom pah pah	93	The mocking bird
67	Frère Jacques	94	Let's call the whole thing off
68	You are my sunshine	95	Strawberry Fair
69	Linstead Market	96	South American tune
70	Dance of the reed flutes	97	Amazing grace
71	Three crows	98	Khayana
72	Clementine	99	Summertime
73	Pennsylvania 6-5000	100	Portsmouth
74	Dance	101	Swing low, sweet chariot
(75	El condor pasa)	102	The bird-catcher's song
76	Melody	103	Gabriel's message
77	American patrol	104	Country gardens
(78	Santa Lucia)	105	I do like to be beside the seaside
79	I wonder as I wander	106	German dance
(80	Silent night)	107	Row weel, my boatie
(81	Dance of the street urchins)	108	The entertainer
82	Brown girl in the ring	(109	My grandfather's clock)
83	Sans Day carol	110	La donn' è mobile
84	Tina singu	(111	O little one sweet)
85	Huntsmen's chorus	(112	Minuet)
86	Ta-ra-ra boom-de-ay		Index of titles

1 Suo-gân

words: Percy Dearmer
music: traditional Welsh

Win - ter creeps, Na - ture sleeps, Birds are gone, Flowers are none.

2 Au clair de la lune

French

3 The old shepherd

L H Page

4 Spring time

Malcolm Pollock

Daf - fo - dils and cro - cus - es, Bright and breez - y, bright and breez - y,

Daf - fo - dils and cro - cus - es, Tell us win - ter's o - ver.

5 Clown dance

French

sim.

6 Andrew mine, Jasper mine

words: C K Offer
music: Moravian carol

An-drew mine, Jas-per mine, Ti-mo-thy and A-bel, Hur-ry to Beth-le-hem, to the com-mon sta-ble.

7 Rigadoon

Purcell

8 Fais do-do

French

9 Folk song

German

10 Apples and pears

L H Page

11 The nightingale

German

12 Little John

German

13 When the saints go marching in

traditional

Oh, when the saints go march-ing in,
Oh, when the saints go march-ing in,
I want to be with-in that num-ber
When the saints go march-ing in.

14 Merrily

traditional

Mer-ri-ly we roll a-long, roll a-long, roll a-long.

legato

Mer-ri-ly we roll a-long, all the live-long day.

15 Hot cross buns
traditional

Hot cross buns! Hot cross buns! One a pen-ny, two a pen-ny, hot cross buns!

16 Pease pudding
traditional

Pease pud-ding hot, pease pud-ding cold. Pease pud-ding in the pot, nine days old.

17 Fais do-do
French

18 Roses from the South

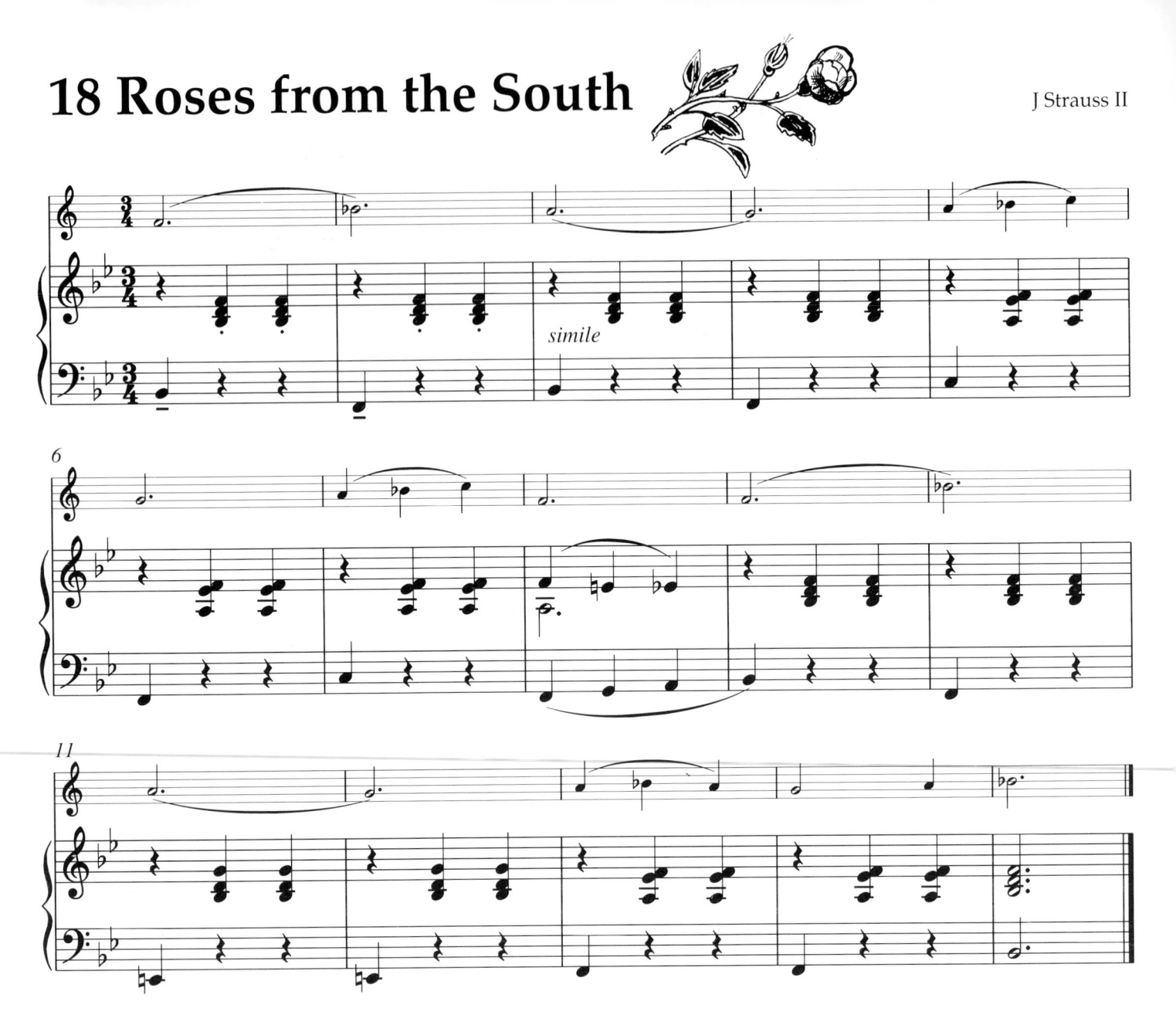

J Strauss II

19 Twinkle, twinkle little star

words: Jane Taylor
music: traditional

Twin - kle, twin - kle lit - tle star, How I won - der what you are.

Up a - bove the world so high, Like a dia - mond in the sky,

Twin-kle, twin-kle lit-tle star, How I won-der what you are.

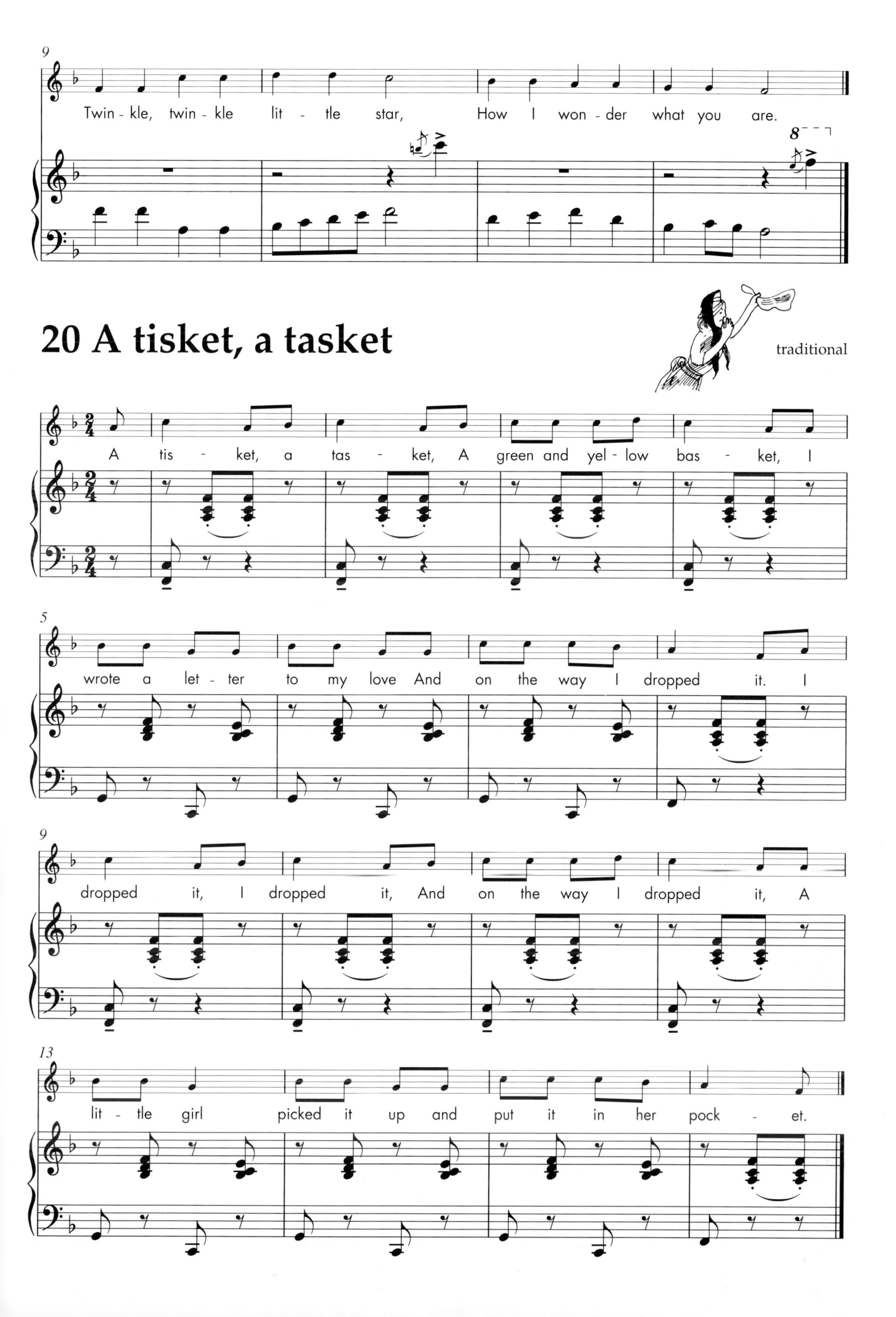

20 A tisket, a tasket

traditional

A tis-ket, a tas-ket, A green and yel-low bas-ket, I wrote a let-ter to my love And on the way I dropped it. I dropped it, I dropped it, And on the way I dropped it, A lit-tle girl picked it up and put it in her pock-et.

21 Southwell

from Damon's Psalter

22 Hatikvah

traditional Hebrew

con Ped.

23 The mocking bird song

North American

Hush little baby, don't say a word, Papa's gonna buy you a mocking bird,
If that mocking bird don't sing, Papa's gonna buy you a diamond ring.

24 Turn the glasses over

traditional

I've been to Harlem I've been to Dover, I've travel'd this wide world all over, O-ver, o-ver, three times over, Drink what you have to drink and turn the glasses over.

The accompaniment fits when the piece is played both as a round and as a solo – repeat the last two bars of accompaniment as necessary until the last player has finished.
* Entry point when played as a round.

25 Annie's song

John Denver

26 The holly and the ivy

traditional

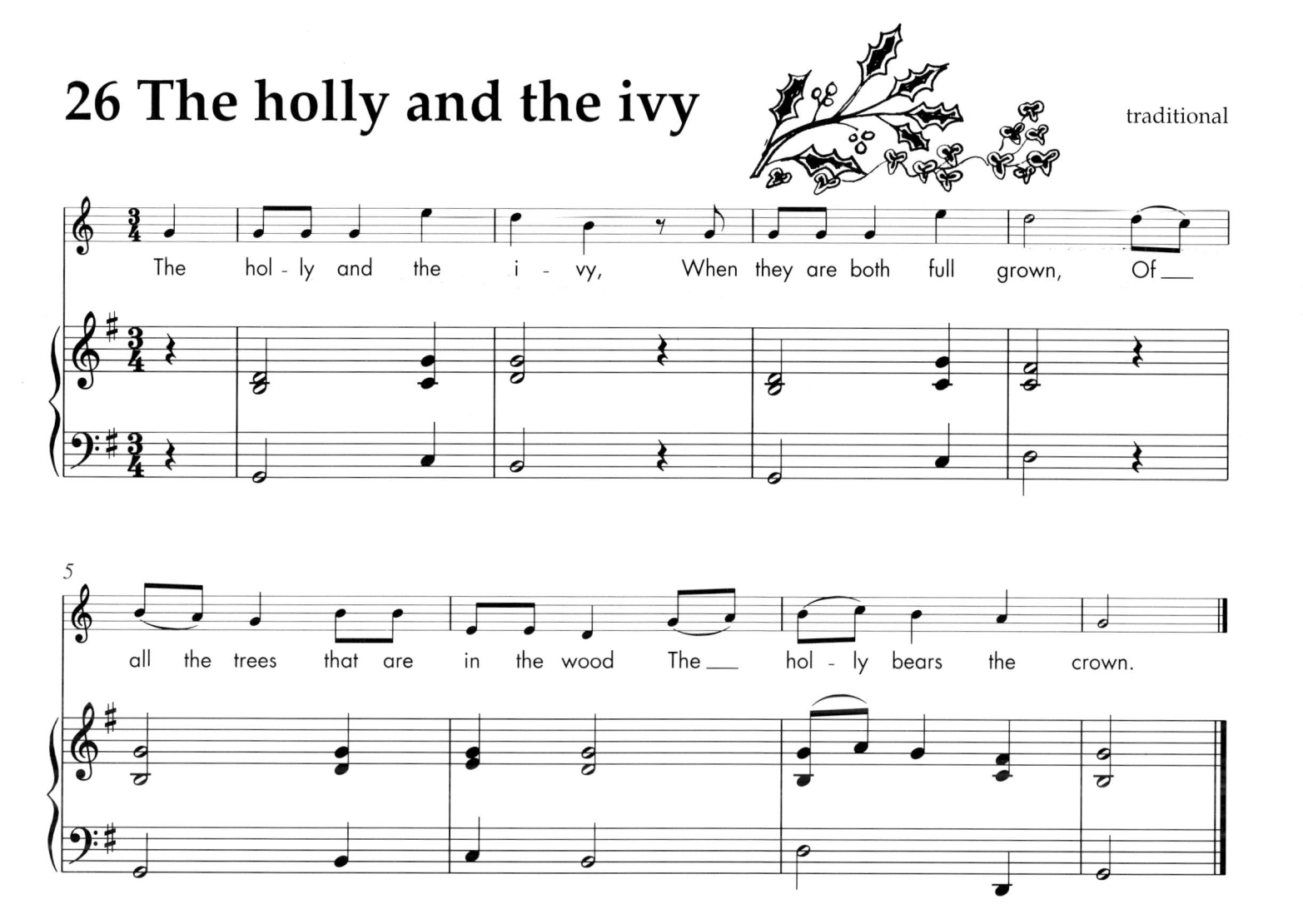

The hol-ly and the i-vy, When they are both full grown, Of all the trees that are in the wood The hol-ly bears the crown.

27 Mr Frog's wedding

North American

28 Away in a manger

W J Kirkpatrick

A-way in a manger, no crib for a bed, The little Lord Jesus laid down His sweet head, The stars in the bright sky looked down where he lay, The little Lord Jesus a-sleep on the hay.

29 Johnny Todd

traditional

Johnny Todd, he took a notion, For to

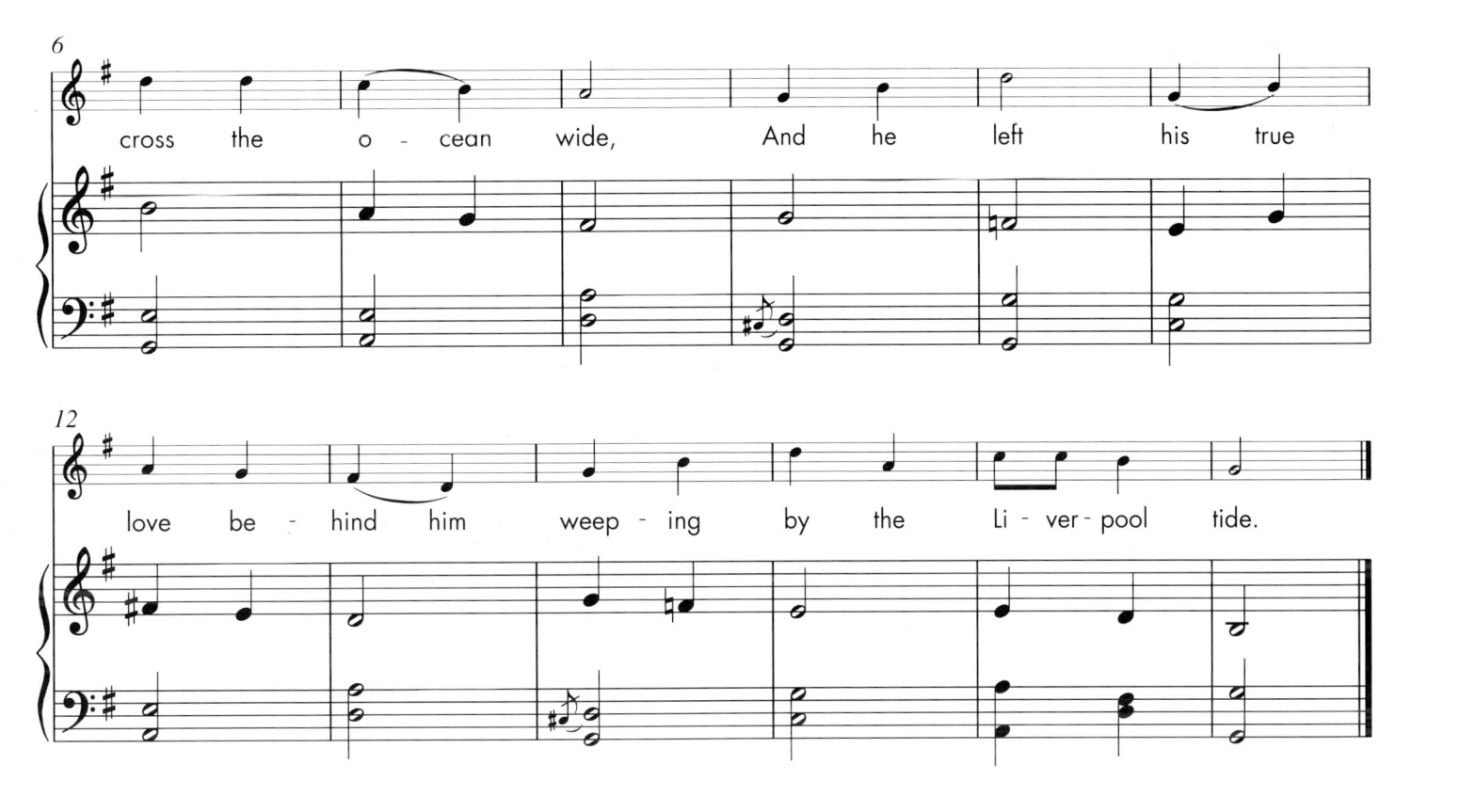

cross the o-cean wide, And he left his true love be-hind him weep-ing by the Li-ver-pool tide.

30 God save the Queen

traditional

Maestoso

31 Ye banks and braes

Scottish

32 Thank U very much

Michael McGear

Thank U ve-ry much for the Ain-tree I-ron, Thank U ve-ry much, Thank U ve-ry, ve-ry, ve-ry much,

Thank U ve-ry much for the Ain-tree I-ron Thank U ve-ry, ve-ry, ve-ry much.

33 Morningtown ride - *unaccompanied duet*

34 Scarborough Fair

traditional

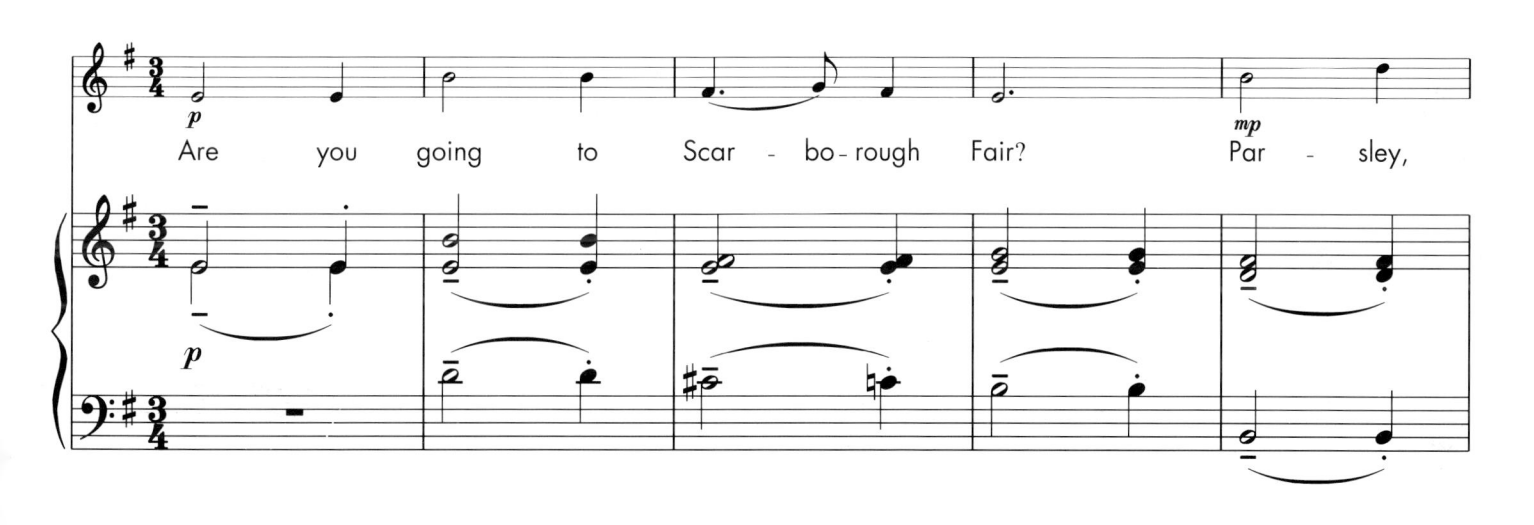

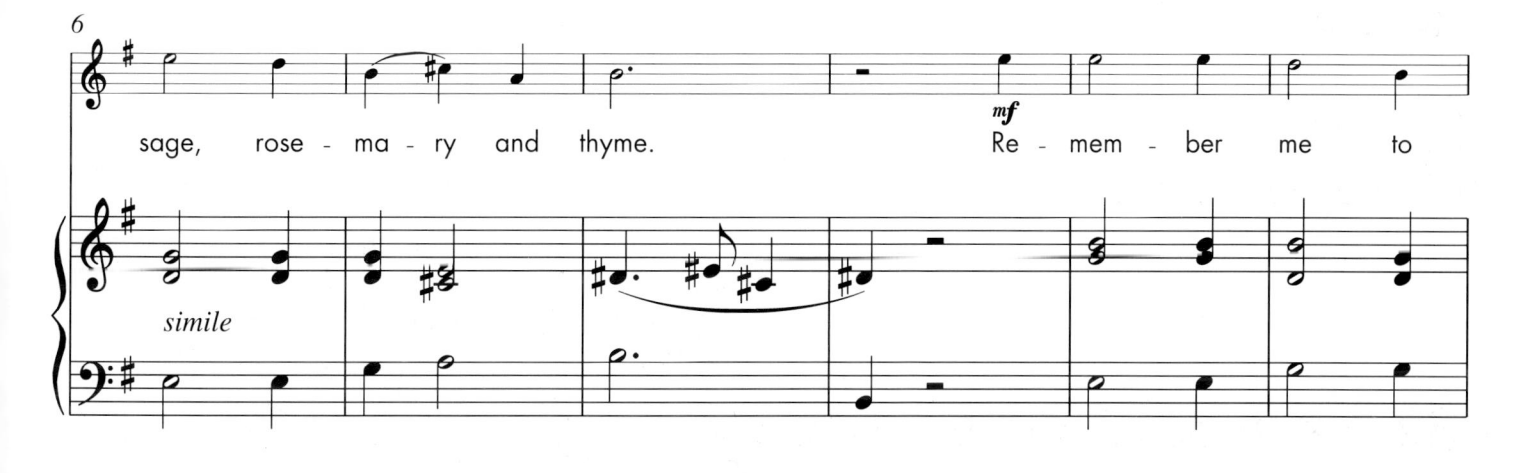

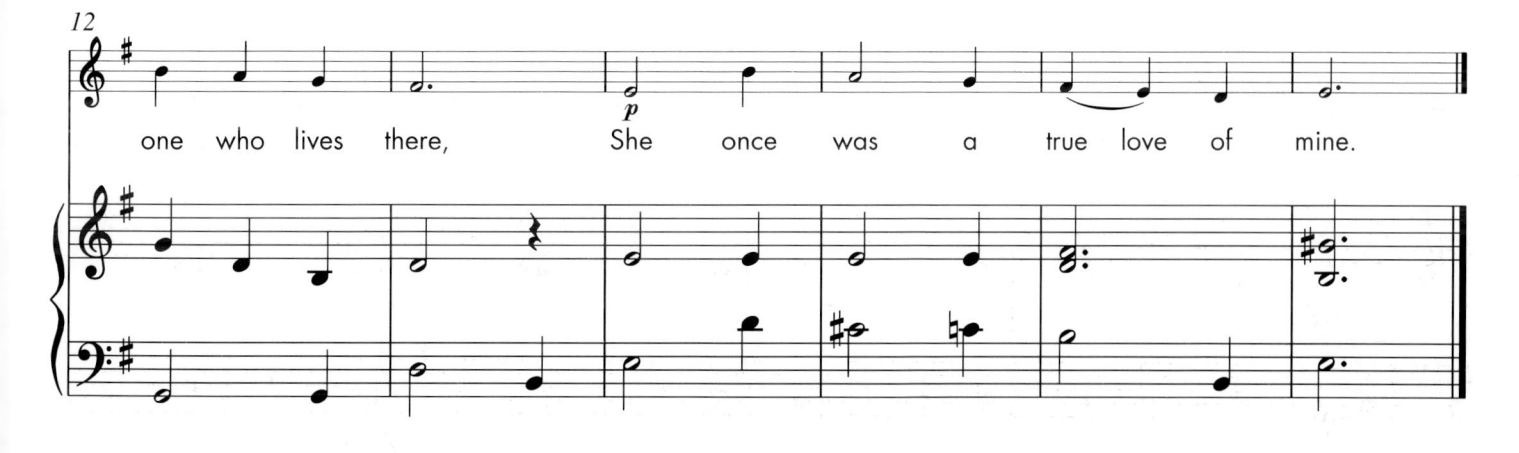

Are you going to Scar-bo-rough Fair? Par-sley, sage, rose-ma-ry and thyme. Re-mem-ber me to one who lives there, She once was a true love of mine.

35 Shepherds' hey

traditional

36 Old MacDonald

traditional

Old Mac-Do-nald had a farm, E - I - E - I - O! And on that farm he had some flutes, E - I - E - I - O! With a

37 Waiting

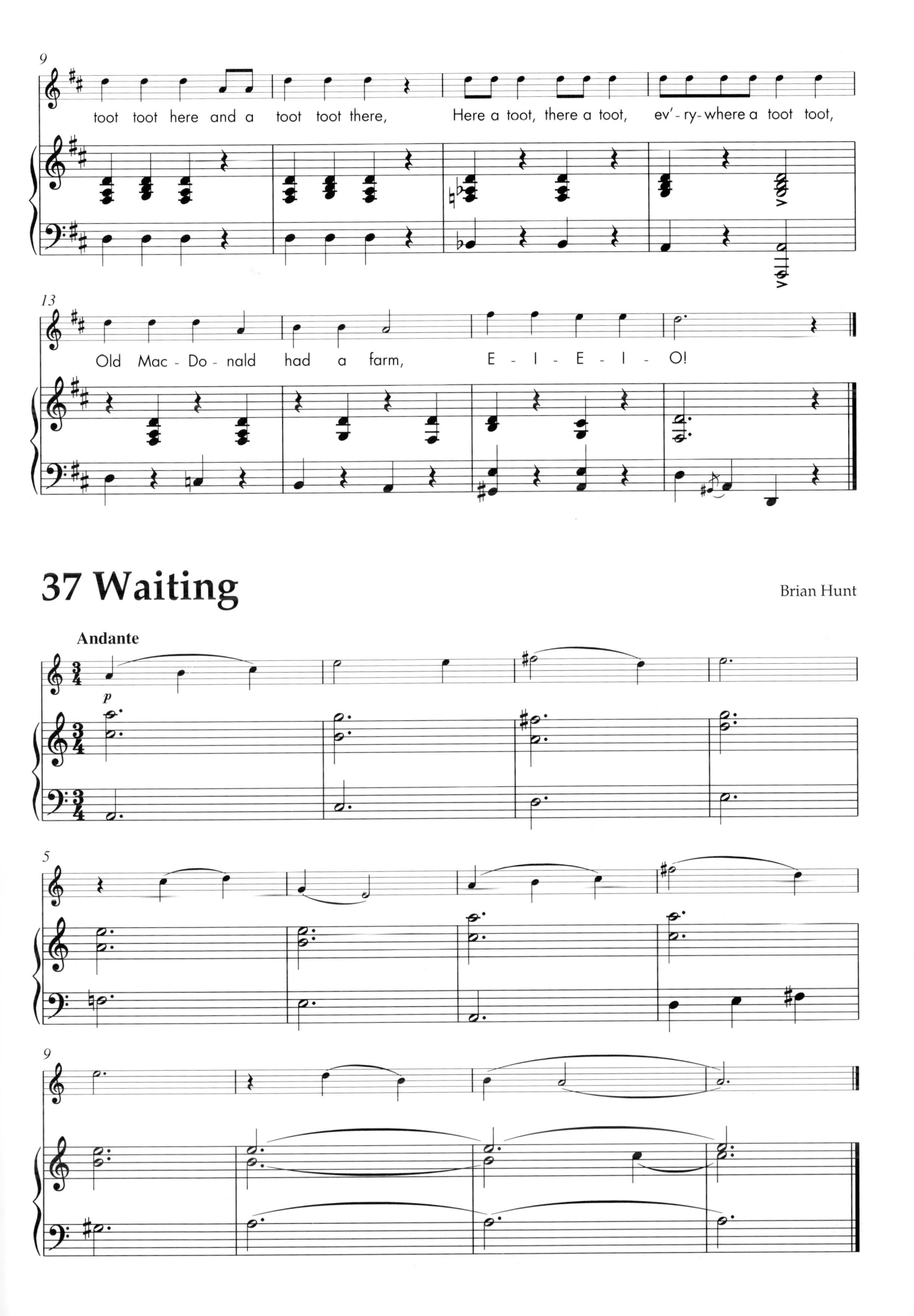

Brian Hunt

Andante

38 Fishermen's song

Ecuador

Allegro

leggiero

39 Chimes at night

Chinese

40 Kookaburra

Australian

Koo-ka-bur-ra sits on an old gum tree___ Mer-ry mer-ry King of the bush is he;___ Laugh, koo-ka-bur-ra laugh, koo-ka-bur-ra, Gay your life must be.

The accompaniment fits when the piece is played both as a round and as a solo – repeat the last two bars of accompaniment as necessary until the last player has finished.
* Entry point when played as a round.

41 Quem pastores

German

Moderato

42 Love song - *unaccompanied duet*

43 Come and sing together

Hungarian

The accompaniment fits when the piece is played both as a round and as a solo – repeat the last two bars of accompaniment as necessary until the last player has finished.
* Entry point when played as a round.

44 Dublin bay

traditional

45 The bear went over the mountain

traditional

The bear went o-ver the moun - tain, The bear went o-ver the moun - tain, The bear went o-ver the moun - tain To see what he could see. And all that he could see, And all that he could see, Was the o - ther side of the moun - tain, The o - ther side of the moun - tain, The o - ther side of the moun - tain Was all that he could see.

46 Barcarolle - *unaccompanied duet*

47 Summer is icumen in

Mediaeval English

The accompaniment fits when the piece is played both as a round and as a solo – repeat the last two bars of accompaniment as necessary until the last player has finished.
* Entry point when played as a round.

48 Morning has broken

words: Eleanor Farjeon
music: Gaelic

Morn-ing has bro - ken   Like the first morn - ing,   Black-bird has spo - ken   Like the first bird.

Praise for the sing - ing!   Praise for the morn - ing!   Praise for them, spring - ing   Fresh from the Word!

49 Over the hills and far away

traditional

50 Rakes of Mallow

traditional

51 Theme from the *'Surprise' Symphony*

Haydn

52 O mio babbino caro

Puccini

53 Plaisir d'amour

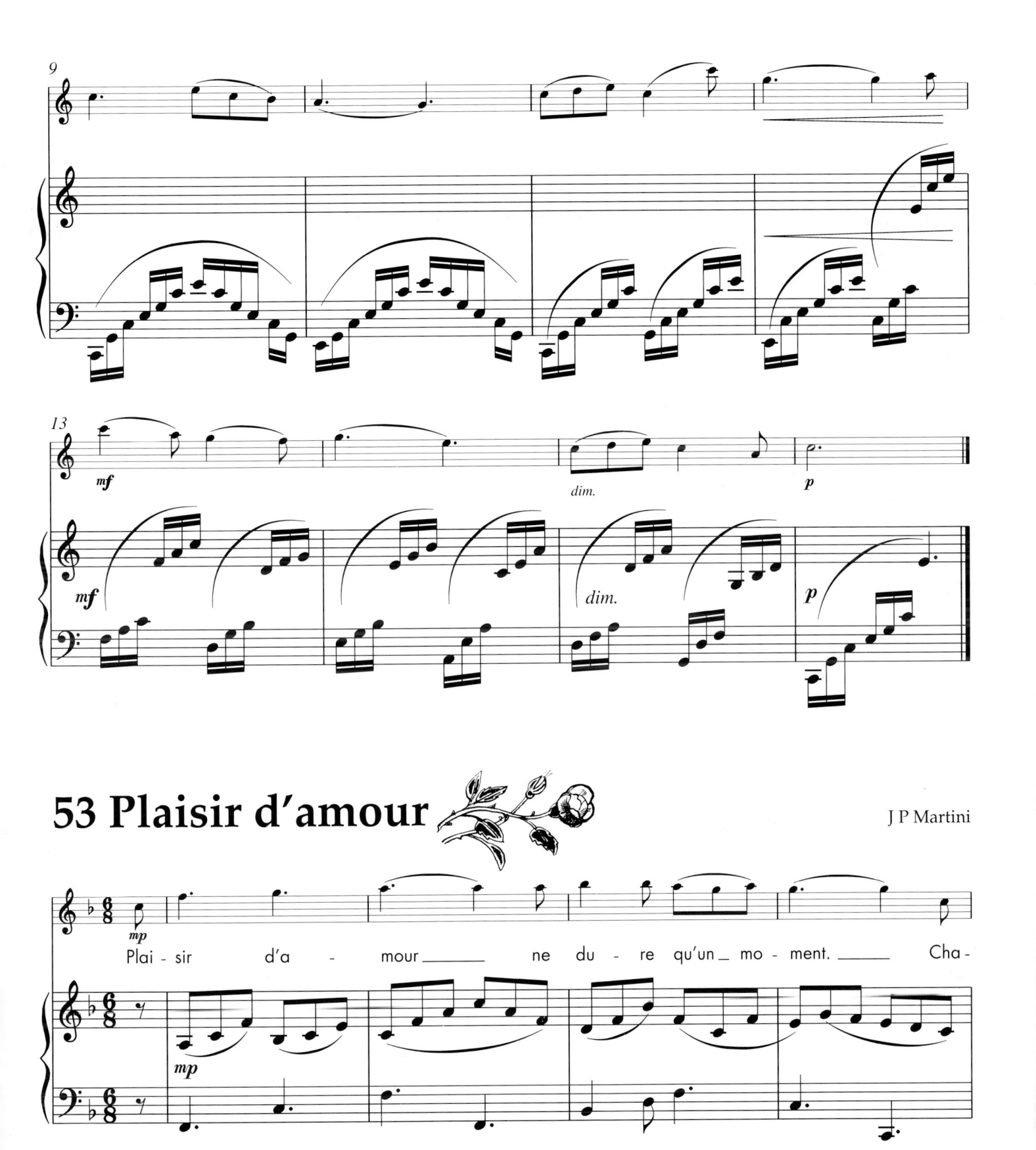

J P Martini

Plai - sir d'a - mour ne du - re qu'un mo - ment. Cha-grin d'a - mour du - re toute la vie.

54 Listen to the mocking bird

Caribbean

55 Deck the hall

Welsh

Deck the hall with boughs of hol-ly, Fa-la-la-la-la, Fa-la-la-la.

'Tis the sea-son to be jol-ly, Fa-la-la-la-la, Fa-la-la-la.

Fill the mead cup, drain the bar-rel, Fa-la-la-la-la, la-la-la.

Troll the an-cient Christ-mas ca-rol, Fa-la-la-la-la, Fa-la-la-la.

56 O little one sweet

S Scheidt

57 Greensleeves

English

Allegretto

58 Where is love?

Lionel Bart

Where ___ is love? Does it fall from skies a - bove?

Is it un - der - neath the wil - low tree ___ That I've been dream - ing of?

(2nd. time)

59 The moon over the ruined castle

Taki

60 Minka

Russian

Andante

61 Brother James' air

J L M Bain

62 Little brown jug

North American

My wife and I lived all a-lone in a lit-tle log hut we called our own.

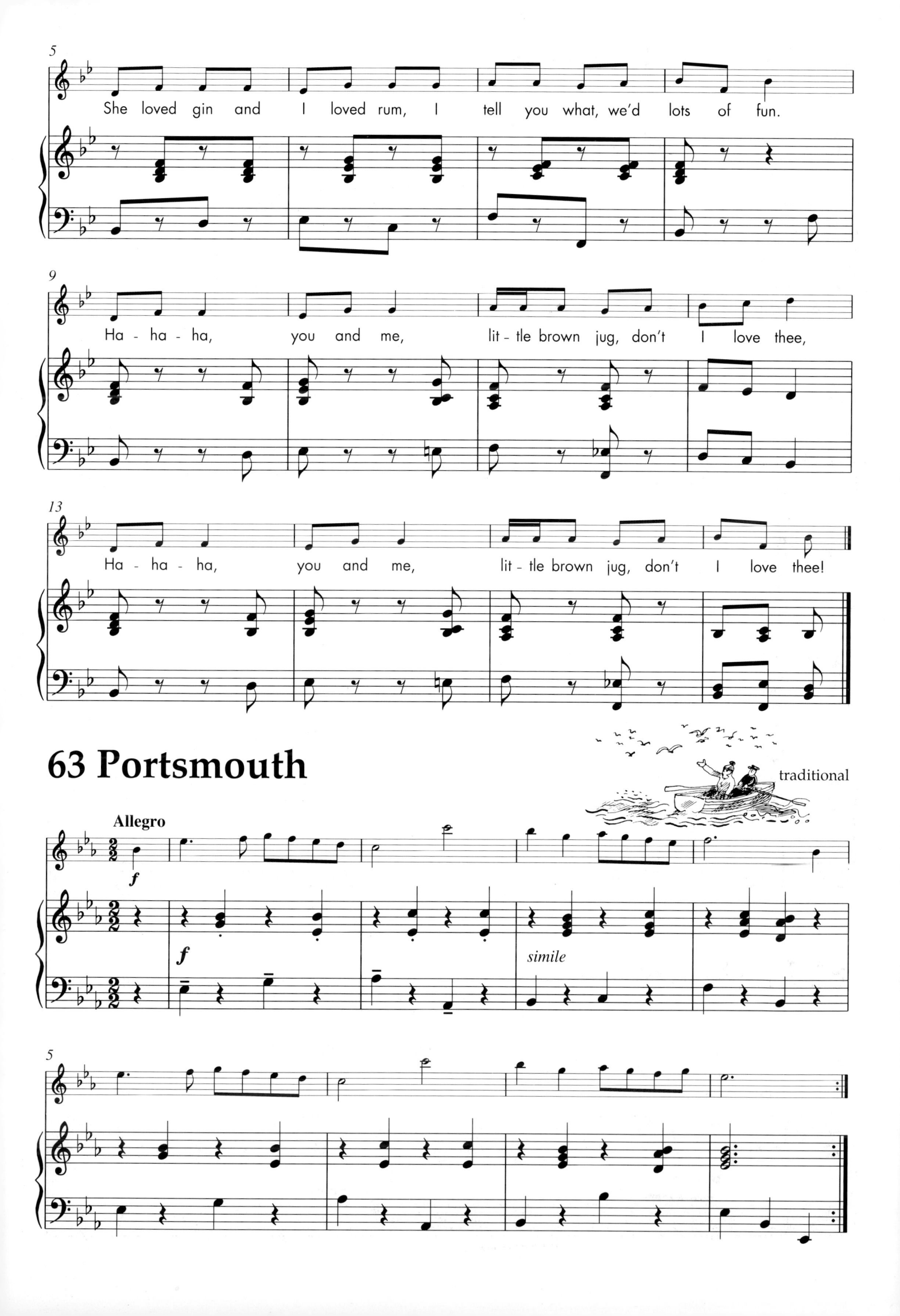

She loved gin and I loved rum, I tell you what, we'd lots of fun.

Ha - ha - ha, you and me, lit - tle brown jug, don't I love thee,

Ha - ha - ha, you and me, lit - tle brown jug, don't I love thee!

63 Portsmouth

traditional

Allegro

64 Huron Indian carol

Canadian

65 Hey, little bull

words: A H Green
music: Brazilian carol

Hey, lit-tle bull be-hind the gate, What are you do-ing up so late? And, lit-tle bull, what have you seen On this starry Christ-mas Eve? If you raise your eyes to hea-ven You will see the Vir-gin's Son, He is clothed in white ap-par-el And is bles-sing ev'-ry-one. La-la-la-la-la la la la la La la lu la-la la-la-la-la-la, La-la-la-la-la la la la la La la-la la-la la la la.

66 Oom pah pah

Lionel Bart

There's a little ditty they're singing in the city, Especially when they've been on the gin or the beer; If you've got the patience your own imaginations will tell you just exactly what you want to hear.

Oom pah pah, oom pah pah, that's how it goes,

Oom pah pah, oom pah pah, eve-ry-one knows.

They all sup-pose what they want to sup-pose

When they hear 'oom pah pah.'

67 Frère Jacques

French

Frè-re Jac-ques, Frè-re Jac-ques, Dor-mez vous? Dor-mez-vous?

Son-nez les ma-ti-nes! Son-nez les ma-ti-nes! Ding, dang, dong! Ding, dang, dong!

The accompaniment fits when the piece is played both as a round and as a solo – repeat the last two bars of accompaniment as necessary until the last player has finished.
* Entry point when played as a round.

68 You are my sunshine

Jimmy Davis/Carl Mitchell

You are my sun-shine, my on-ly sun-shine,

You make me hap-py when skies are grey,

You'll ne-ver know dear, how much I love you,

please don't take my sun-shine a-way.

69 Linstead Market

Jamaican

Car-ry me ack - ie, go a Lin-stead mar-ket, Not a quat - tie would sell.

Car-ry me ack - ie, go a Lin-stead mar-ket, Not a quat - tie would sell.

Lord, not a mite, not a bite, What a Sat - ur-day night!

Lord, not a mite, not a bite, What a Sat - ur-day night!

70 Dance of the reed flutes

Tchaikovsky

Small notes are optional

71 Three crows

Scottish

Three crows sat up-on a wa' Sat up-on a

wa', sat up-on a wa'. _____ Three crows sat up-on a wa' on a cold and frost-y morn-ing.

72 Clementine

North American

Oh my dar-ling, oh my dar-ling, oh my dar-ling Clem-en-tine, Thou art lost and gone for e-ver, dread-ful sor-ry Clem-en-tine.

73 Pennsylvania 6-5000

Sigman/Gray

74 Dance

Boismortier

75 El condor pasa - *unaccompanied duet.*

76 Melody

Rubinstein

77 American patrol

F W Meacham

78 Santa Lucia - *unaccompanied duet*

79 I wonder as I wander

traditional

I wonder as I wander, out under the sky How

Je - sus the sa - viour did come for to die For poor or'n'ry peo - ple like you and like I... I won - der as I wan - der, out un - der the sky.

80 Silent night - *unaccompanied duet*
81 Dance of the street urchins - *unaccompanied duet*

82 Brown girl in the ring

Caribbean

There's a brown girl in the ring, tra-la-la-la-la, There's a brown girl in the ring, tra-la-la-la-la, There's a brown girl in the ring, tra-la-la-la-la, For she like su-gar and I like plum.

83 Sans Day carol

Cornish

Allegro

Now the hol-ly bears a ber-ry as white as the milk, And Ma-ry bore Je-sus who was wrapped up in silk. And Ma-ry bore Je-sus Christ our Sa-viour for to be And the first tree in the green-wood it was the hol-ly, hol-ly, hol-ly, And the first tree in the green-wood it was the hol-ly.

84 Tina singu

African

85 Huntsmen's chorus

Weber

86 Ta-ra-ra boom-de-ay

Harry Sayers

87 Last of the summer wine

Ronnie Hazlehurst

88 March of the kings

French

Allegro moderato

89 Londonderry air

traditional

90 Tambourin

Gossec

91 Theme from the *'New World' Symphony*

Dvořák

92 Mango walk

traditional

My brother did a tell me that you go mango walk. You go mango walk. You go mango walk, My brother did a tell me that you go mango walk And steal all the number 'leven.

Now tell me Joe do tell me for true, Do tell me for true, do tell me That you don't go to no mango walk And steal all the number 'leven.

93 The mocking bird

Haitian

Allegretto

Have you heard the song of the mocking bird?

Have you heard the song of the mocking bird?

When you sad and blue, Then he mock at you, He sing high above, And he laugh at love.

Oh I heard his tune By the Haitian moon, When I lost my Choucoune.

94 Let's call the whole thing off

Gershwin

95 Strawberry Fair

traditional

As I was going to Strawberry Fair, Ri - fol, ri - fol, tol - de - rid - dle - li - do I met a mai - den sell - ing her ware, fol - de - dee. I met a mai - den sell - ing her ware As she went on to Straw - ber - ry Fair. Ri - fol, ri - fol, tol - de - rid - dle - li - do, Ri - fol, ri - fol, tol - de - rid - dle - dee.

96 South American tune

folk melody

97 Amazing grace

words: John Newton
music: traditional

A - ma - zing grace, how sweet the sound that saved a wretch like me, I once was lost but now am found, was blind but now I see. 'Twas grace that taught my heart to fear, and grace my fears re-lieved. How precious did that grace appear the hour I first believed.

98 Khayana

Gujarati

99 Summertime

Gershwin

100 Portsmouth

traditional

101 Swing low, sweet chariot

spiritual

Swing low, sweet chariot, coming for to carry me home, Swing low, sweet chariot, coming for to carry me home. I looked over Jordan and what did I see, coming for to carry me home? A band of angels *coming after me,__ coming for to carry me home.*

Swing low, sweet chariot__ coming for to carry me home,

Swing low, sweet chariot__ coming for to carry me home.

morendo
Coming for to carry me home.__

102 The bird-catcher's song

Mozart

Moderato

103 Gabriel's message

traditional Basque

104 Country gardens

morris tune

Allegro

105 I do like to be beside the seaside

John A Glover-Kind

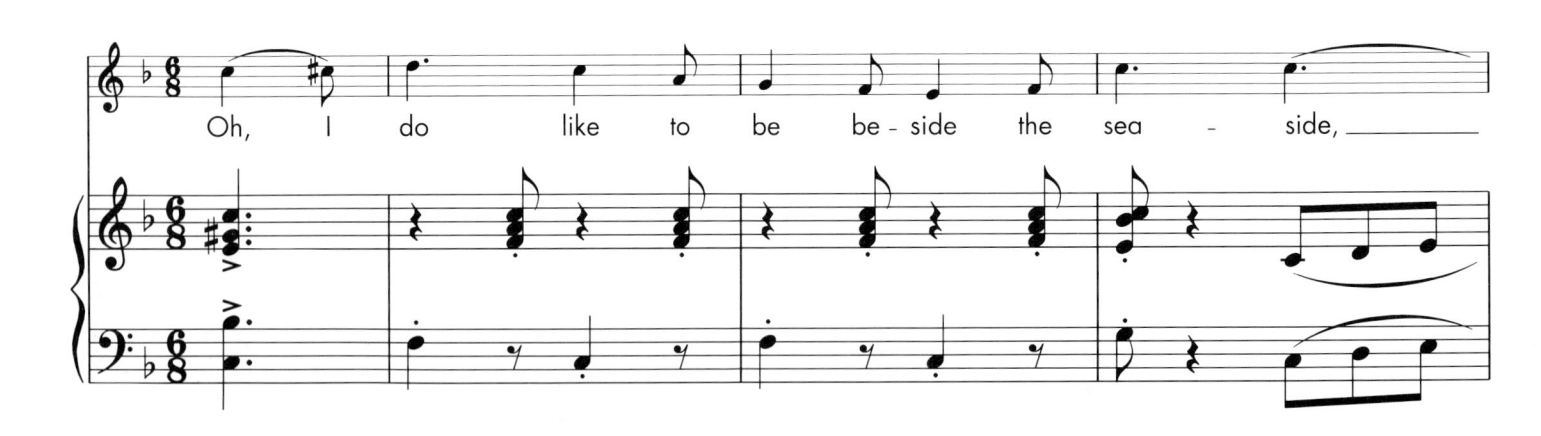

Oh, I do like to be be-side the sea - side,

4
Oh, I do like to be be-side the sea. I
simile
9
do like to stroll up-on the prom, prom, prom, where the brass bands play, Tid-de-ly-
15
om - pom - pom! So just let me be be-side the sea - side,
21
I'll be be-side my-self with glee; And there's lots of girls be-sides, I should
27
like to be be-side, Be-side the sea - side, Be-side the sea.

106 German dance

Mozart

Allegro moderato

107 Row weel, my boatie

Scottish

108 The entertainer

Scott Joplin

109 My grandfather's clock - *unaccompanied duet*

110 La donn'è mobile

Verdi

111 O little sweet one - *unaccompanied trio*
112 Minuet - *unaccompanied trio*

Index of titles

Titles in brackets are unaccompanied and are not included in this volume.

A tisket, a tasket, 20
Amazing grace, 97
American patrol, 77
Andrew mine, Jasper mine, 6
Annie's song, 25
Apples and pears, 10
Au clair de la lune, 2
Away in a manger, 28

(BAGs, Warm up 1) (before 1)
(Barcarolle (duet), 46)
Bear went over the mountain, The 45
Bird-catcher's song, The 102
Brother James' air, 61
Brown girl in the ring, 82

(CABs, Warm up 3) (before 5)
(Caves, Warm up 6) (before 9)
(CDs, Warm up 8) (before 19)
Chimes at night, 39
Clementine, 72
Clown dance, 5
Come and sing together (round), 43
Country gardens, 104

Dance of the reed flutes, 70
(Dance of the street urchins (duet), 81)
Dance, 74
Deck the hall, 55
(Don't look now!, Warm up 17) (before 59)
Dublin bay, 44

(El condor pasa (duet), 75)
Entertainer, The 108

(F♯ workout, Warm up 12) (before 28)
Fais do-do, 8, 17
Fishermen's song, 38
(Flying high, Warm up 15) (before 50)
Folk song, 9
Frère Jacques (round), 67

(G whizz, Warm up 13) (before 31)
Gabriel's message, 103
German dance, 106
God save the Queen, 30
(Good DEED, Warm up 10) (before 21)
Greensleeves, 57

Hatikvah, 22
Hey, little bull, 65
(His 'n' hers slurs, Warm up 7) (before 17)
Holly and the ivy, The 26
Hot cross buns, 15
(How's your father?, Warm up 18) (before 62)
Huntsmen's chorus, 85
Huron Indian carol, 64

I wonder as I wander, 79
I do like to be beside the seaside, 105

Johnny Todd (duet), 29

Khayana, 98
Kookaburra (round), 40

La donn'è mobile, 110
Last of the summer wine, 87
(Lazing (duet), Warm up 2) (before 5)
Let's call the whole thing off, 94
Linstead Market, 69
Listen to the mocking bird, 54
(Little finger workout, Warm up 20) (before 84)
Little John, 12
Little brown jug, 62
Londonderry air, 89

(Love song (duet), 42)
Mango walk, 92
March of the kings, 88
Melody, 76
Merrily, 14
Minka, 60
(Minuet (trio), 112)
Mocking bird, The 93
Mocking bird song, The 23
Moon over the ruined castle, The 59
Morning has broken, 48
(Morningtown Ride (duet), 33)
Mr Frog's wedding, 27
(My grandfather's clock (duet), 109)

Nightingale, The 11

O mio babbino caro, 52
O little one sweet (trio), 111
O little one sweet, 56
Old MacDonald (duet), 36
Old shepherd, The 3
Oom pah pah, 66
(Oranges and lemons (duet), Warm up 9) (before 20)
Over the hills and far away, 49

Pease pudding (duet), 16
Pennsylvania 6-5000, 73
Plaisir d'amour, 53
Portsmouth, 63
Portsmouth (in D), 100

Quem pastores, 41

Rakes of Mallow, 50
Rigadoon, 7
(Rolling hills, Warm up 16) (before 56)
Roses from the South, 18
Row weel, my boatie, 107

Sans Day carol, 83
(Santa Lucia (duet), 78)
Scarborough Fair, 34
(Sharp CDs, Warm up 14) (before 33)
Shepherds' hey, 35
(Silent night (duet), 80)
(Soaring, Warm up 19) (before 67)
South American tune, 96
Southwell, 21
Spring time, 4
Strawberry Fair, 95
Summer is icumen in (round), 47
Summertime, 99
Suo-gân, 1
(Suo-gân (in C), Warm up 11) (before 26)
Swing low, sweet chariot, 101

Ta-ra-ra boom-de-ay, 86
Tambourin, 90
Thank U very much, 32
Theme from the New World Symphony, 91
Theme from Surprise Symphony, 51
Three crows, 71
Tina singu, 84
Turn the glasses over (round), 24
Twinkle, twinkle little star, 19
(Two flutes together (duet), Warm up 4) (before 9)

Waiting, 37
(Waves, Warm up 5) (before 9)
When the saints go marching in (duet), 13
Where is love?, 58

Ye banks and braes, 31
You are my sunshine, 68

Acknowledgements

All arrangements are by Jane Sebba except 37 by Brian Hunt, 38 by Malcolm Pollock and 59, 84, 96, and 98 by David Moses.

The following have kindly granted permission for the reprinting of copyright material:

Andrew Mine, Jasper Mine and **Hey little bull** © Oxford University Press 1962 and 1966. Used by permission.

Annie's song, words and music by John Denver. Copyright © 1974 Cherry Lane Music Publishing Inc, (ASCAP) and DreamWorks (ASCAP). Worldwide rights for DreamWorks administered by Cherry Lane Music Publishing Company Inc. International Copyright Secured. All Rights Reserved.

Last of the summer wine, © Ronnie Hazlehurst Ms.

Let's call the whole thing off, music and lyrics by George Gershwin and Ira Gershwin © 1936, 1937 (renewed 1963, 1964) George Gershwin Music and Ira Gershwin Music. All rights administered by WB Music Corp, USA. Warner/Chappell Music Ltd, London W6 8BS. All rights reserved.

Morning has broken, words by Eleanor Farjeon, David Higham Associates, taken from Eleanor Farjeon's 'The Children's Bells'. Published by Oxford University Press.

Pennsylvania 6-5000, words and music by Jerry Gray and Carl Sigman © 1940 EMI Catalogue Partnership/EMI Robbins Catalog Inc. USA. Worldwide print rights controlled by Warner Bros Inc. USA/IMP Ltd. All Rights Reserved. Reproduced by permission of IMP Ltd.

Summertime, music and lyrics by George Gershwin, Du Bose, Dorothy Heyward and Ira Gershwin © 1935 (renewed 1962) George Gershwin Music, Ira Gershwin Music and Du Bose and Dorothy Heyward Memorial Fund. All rights administered by WB Music Corp, USA. Warner/Chappell Music Ltd, London W6 8BS All rights reserved. Reproduced by permission of International Music Publications.

Thank U very much, words and music by Michael McGear. © Copyright 1967 Noel Gay Music Company Ltd, 8/9 Frith Street London, W1. Used by permission of Music Sales Ltd. All rights reserved. International Copyright secured.

Waiting Brian Hunt.

Where is love? and **Oom pah pah**, words and music by Lionel Bart © 1960 Lakeview Music Publishing Co Ltd, Suite 2.07, Plaza 535 Kings Road, London SW10 0SZ. International copyright secured. All Rights Reserved. Used by Permission.

You are my sunshine, words and music by Jimmie Davis and Charles Mitchell. © copyright 1940 Peer International corporation USA. Peermusic (UK) Limited, 8-14 Verulam Street, London WC1. Used by permission of Music Sales Ltd. All rights reserved. International Copyright Secured.

All other items © A&C Black.